Traditional Sun Lu-T'ang Style Taijiquan

1957 Guidebook *by* Madam Sun Jian-Yun
(Daughter *of* Grandmaster Sun Lu-T'ang)

Photographic Guidebook:
95 ~ Posture Form

Compiled *&* Translated *by*
Bradford Tyrey

Find more of our publications at:

www.neijiabooks.com

Beloved Dedication to:

My beloved parents: Alan & Marguerite.
Master Sun Lu-T'ang's daughter: Madam Sun Jian-Yun.
Master Sun Lu-T'ang's disciple: Master Wang Xi-Kui.
Master Sun Lu-T'ang's grandson: Master Sun Bao-An.
Master Liu Bin's and Master Sun Lu-T'ang's student: Master Liu Xing-Han.
The family of Master Sun Lu-T'ang's disciple: Master Jue Hau.
Master Cheng Bing-Jun:
Monk T'ang-I: disciple of many of the great masters.
Madam Wang Ju-Rong [Master Wang Zi-Ping's daughter] & Dr. Wu Cheng-De.
Master Sha Guo-Zhen [Zheng].
Master Liang Ke-Quan.
Master Fu Zhong-Wen.
General He'r Swei-Ding: disciple under several of Sun Lu-Tang's disciples.
All be blessed and rest in eternal peace.

Special Dedication to:

Dave Martin: a long-time student and revered disciple under Madam Sun Jian-Yun.
Su-Ying Martin: a revered and dedicated student under Madam Sun Jian-Yun.
Tony Kansarns: a long-time student under Dave Martin.
Carl Bateman: long-time student under Dave Martin and Zhang Zhen-Hua.
Dorothy Bateman: long-time student under Dave Martin.
Sean Muttaqi: student under Master Liu Xing-Han, Master Liang Ke-Quan and Bradford Tyrey.

United Kingdom: The following instructors recognize the contribution of Dave Martin, and continue his dedication to Madam Sun Jian-Yun in actively teaching Sun style Taijiquan in the United Kingdom and Canary Isles at present:
Carl Bateman, Dorothy Bateman, Harvey Chesshire, Gilda James, Haydn James, John Jones, Gloria Lake, Don Morgan, Sue Murfin, Isabel Perez-Comet (Tenerife, Canary Islands), Zaya Hernandez-Reyes (Tenerife, Canary Islands), Wendy Sutcliffe, and Ken Webster.

USA: Students under Bradford Tyrey in order of seniority:
Sean Muttaqi, Tirk Wilder, Rex Wycherley, Professor Peter Barker (University of Oklahoma), Harold Proske, Joseph McCann, Thomas Meadows, James Ashby, Chen Ming, Kirsten Killinger, Chimene Long, Trudi Pye, Myles Martin, Elijah Martin, Curtis Martin, Scott Starwalt, Evan Espinoza, and Keith Gibson.

Introduction

My introduction to the practices of Master Sun Lu-T'ang occurred in 1984 when I was, by chance, visiting a historian who was teaching at *Bei Da* (Beijing University). Through our talks he mentioned that he had been studying *taijiquan* and other arts with Madam Sun Jian-Yun, daughter of Sun Lu-T'ang. I immediately asked, rather, begged him for an introduction, and within a week I was given permission to visit her class.

Madam Sun was one of those rare teachers who not only embraced a wide body of knowledge, but also deeply cared about her students. She held family, students and friends close to her, always with softly spoken words. These qualities, she said, she learned from her father.

Beginning my studies with Madam Sun in 1984 placed me as one of the first western students to study with her on a somewhat consistent basis. I know of only one other private student who was western who trained with Madam Sun during that time, Timothy Hood, from Ireland, who had been studying with her for nearly eight months prior to my arrival.

The photo above shows, Madam Sun Jian-Yun, one of her students who later became Madam Sun's personal assistant, and myself (Bradford Tyrey), pose for a photo immediately following class at the little park near her apartment in Spring, 1992. Madam Sun said this was an important photo because it marked my eighth year of having trained with her. However, she pointed out that I had not acquired eight years of skill, suggesting, in a lighthearted manner, that I begin my studies all over again and endeavor more vigorously this time, reminding me that my apartment in Beijing was only a ten minute brisk walk from her place, therefore I had no excuse for being late for class. Each photo opportunity with Madam Sun meant that a lesson was about to be learned, this time reminding me of my innate laziness and my habitual tardiness for which I was always apologizing. She said that my spoken Chinese was perfect when I said '*Dui bu qi*,' basically 'Forgive Me,' because I had so much practice saying this when I arrived to class late. She was right, the rest of my Chinese was worse than terrible. This was her way of encouraging me to study Chinese with great effort, but it still didn't work, my laziness and wanderlust were my downfall. However, for this photo, Madam Sun told me to place my hand on her shoulder, uncommon in tradition, to show our closeness as teacher and student.

Most of her students lived in her proximity, so I would often encounter them on the streets nearby. Such familiarity helped me to make friends with many, and through such friendship they shared so much with me that Madam Sun had taught years prior to my arrival. A huge part of my knowledge came from tea house discussions with her students where we sat, talked, and ate roasted pumpkin seeds.

From 1984 to 1997 were the years that I received training from Madam Sun and several individuals in the Sun clan. I am the first to say that I was not able to train with her on a daily basis, in fact there were times when I was in Shanghai, another region, or Taiwan for months before returning to her class. After 1997, I returned for visits and training over the years until her passing.

Beyond lectures and classes that Madam Sun provided us with, she introduced many of us to students, still alive, who trained with Sun Lu-T'ang. They were in their nineties, and still practiced each day, whether standing or sitting. They were devoted to the practice of his teachings. From these gentlemen and their students, who lived in Beijing and Nanjing, we were able to acquire further insight into the background, teaching methods, and practices of Sun Lu-T'ang.

My publications: *The Internal Practices of Sun Lu-T'ang* and *Traditional Sun Lu-T'ang Style*: *Questions & Answers* (*Volume I.*), provide an introduction to the explanations and teachings that Madam Sun presented in classes and in private lectures. These books will provide readers with diverse and important information regarding the breadth of traditional Sun teachings and how these teachings directly relate to taijiquan, baguazhang, and xingyiquan.

Lastly, 'Why am I writing these texts?' I simply do not want the teachings of Madam Sun to be lost over time. I am presenting what I was given in her classes and what her students shared with me, all of which are but part of the practices that her father and his masters taught to their students. These writings do not belong to me, but to those of you who search for original methods and practices from Master Sun Lu-T'ang, Madam Sun Jian-Yun, and their devoted students.

Bradford Tyrey

Special Appreciation

A very special thank you must be given to Carl Bateman (cited below) without whose tireless help none of our publications would have seen the light of day.

Dave Martin (far left), disciple under Madam Sun Jian-Yun; Master Zhang Zhen-Hua (a senior disciple under Madam Sun); and Carl Bateman (long-time student under both Dave Martin and Master Zhang).

About This Book

孫劍雲

Madam Sun Jian-Yun (1913-2003),
daughter of Grandmaster Sun Lu-T'ang.

In 1957, Madam Sun had two books published on Sun style taijiquan. The first book covers the 95-posture form and was published by the Chinese government through the People's Press for Physical Education. There were suggestions given to Madam Sun by Party members who ruled over the People's Press as to what they felt should be contained in the book. This is somewhat reflected in the book. The details I will not publish here as Madam Sun felt things eventually came to an encouraging fruition. Privately, Madam Sun published a second book in 1957 that contains all 97 postures as seen in the two pages below. The 97-Posture book became quite popular and was again republished in both 1986 and 1993. In that book, Madam Sun used 201 photos of herself performing the postures contained in the traditional 97-movement form, which was her way to correct the People's Press book in a respectful and diplomatic manner.

Above, two pages from Madam Sun's 1957 self-published, official instructional textbook.

The book that you have in hand is according to how Madam Sun initially taught me postures. She would group certain postures together and explain that these must be learned as a linked set, while other postures must be studied one at a time. I have laid out this book just as Madam Sun had taught our class in 1984 in Beijing. In each class, public or private, she taught both the correct and incorrect methods to perform each posture, and explained special teachings on postures as passed down by her father, Grandmaster Sun Lu-T'ang.

In Madam Sun's 1957 taiji book she provides general details on which direction to turn, foot and hand placement, and explanations of this sort to assist students in rudimentary practice. I plan to publish a future book with the exact translation of her book along with many of the notes that she taught us in class and in private over the years. In this version of her book, I have placed only a few pages of detailed notes scattered throughout to provide you with insight into the deeper aspects of the Sun family arts that Madam Sun said that her father adhered to and taught each of his disciples. As we learned more about each posture over the years many of us found that we had accumulated four or more pages of notes on each posture. This is not, as Madam Sun said, uncommon to traditional arts from old lineages. As all of the Sun taiji postures came from the arts of baguazhang, xingyiquan and taijiquan that her father learned from his masters. These collective teachings were merged within the Sun taiji form. Madam Sun told us that a person could practice Sun taiji without studying baguazhang, xingyiquan or qigong, though to correctly approach and practice her family's taiji at a deeper level these arts must be addressed. Over the years, Madam Sun, Wang Xi-Kui, Liu Xing-Han, Cheng Bing-Jun, Sun Peng, Sun Bao and seniors in the Sun clan taught us that Grandmaster Sun Lu-T'ang's knowledge was very broad and deep, and that his collective knowledge was placed within the forms, training sets and studies that he carefully imparted. In classes we were taught to keep mindful of each posture, its origin from a specific art, where each posture is found within one or more of the three boxing arts mentioned above, the Taoist practices that are embraced, and how to properly nurture qi within each posture in the Sun taiji form.

Lastly, I have added photos below that Madam Sun gave to me and others that I had acquired while in China. She acquired these in Shanghai while there with her father during a teaching engagement. The first photo below was taken in Beijing in the late 1890s. Many of these photographic negatives were taken to Shanghai where developing them was cheaper than in the north. She later found out that two Europeans had a small shop in Shanghai during the late 1800s and into the early 1900s that supplied both medical and photographic supplies, and even operated a tiny studio in a back room for developing negatives. Some of the photos were sold to tourists and shops and were therefore not difficult to acquire. Over many decades Madam Sun collected many photos that showed life as it was in China, the life that she and her parents had both loved and endured.

This photo shows a typical street market in Beijing during the 1890s, where you were served tea, soup and the staple of the day. Hot tea and hot soup meant that the water was safe to drink because boiled water meant that dysentery was less likely. A daily staple that was offered at most outdoor food stalls was mutton and noodles. Madam Sun remarked that she could imagine her father sitting among such a group while drinking tea. She felt that it was important for us to understand that life was both difficult and dangerous for him because as a well-known boxing master her father had been often targeted by gangs, bandits, and those who wanted to harm him in order to make a name for themselves. In the midst of such challenging times Sun Lu-T'ang both studied and developed his family art. Madam Sun wanted all of us to well understand that the taiji that she taught us in a peaceful and secure environment was developed by her father in a time and place that was anything but ideal as a setting for taijiquan.

Madam Sun loved this photo of a young boy who was carrying scraps of metal and brass discarded by shop owners or pieces just found in the street. His job, like many thousands of youth back then, was to carry, in his baskets, anything of some value that he found and bring his daily collection to a scrap vendor. This photo (circa early 1900s) reminded her of her father's days of poverty and starvation when he was young. She said that it is important that no matter whether one is rich or carrying baskets, we must all treat each other with dignity and kindness. As Madam said to all of us, this boy in the photo represents her father and each one of us.

Hangzhou, China (left), near Shanghai, and Loong Hua Pagoda (right), on the outskirts of Hangzhou, as they appeared around 1900. Sun Lu-T'ang conducted classes in Hangzhou beginning in the late 1920s and attended many martial arts ceremonies at Loong Hua Pagoda.

This well-known photo among Sun style enthusiasts shows a gathering of teachers and students at a Heibei Province Guoshu (National Martial Arts) school located in Tianjin, China, 1927, at which Sun Lu-T'ang frequently taught. Students trained at this school were often hired out as bodyguards, cross-land security personnel and neighborhood police officers. Madam Sun explained that although guns were available in those years they were highly restricted by law. Traditional martial arts schools generally taught weaponry (swords, knives, etc.) that was widely available and in use by the general public. She said that this photo shows the common weapons taught in those years at such schools: three-sectioned staff (far left), long knives, spears, swords (center), staff, tiger-hook swords (right side), and bagua big knife (far right).

Sun Lu-T'ang (seated in the middle) with students in his xingyiquan class, Shanxi Province, China, 1924. Madam Sun said that this class was composed of many martial arts masters who wanted to study xingyi and Taoist philosophy from her father. In this 1924 class, as he had with other groups, Master Sun introduced what he simply termed *Bienquan* (Changing Fist [Boxing]), later naming it *Sun Shi Kai-He'r Hua Bu Taijiquan* (Sun style Open-Unite Active Stepping Tai-Chi Boxing).

Sun Lu-T'ang demonstrating 白猿托桃 *Bai Yuan Tuo Tao*
(White Ape Supports [Upholds] Peach) from baguazhang sword.
托 *Tuo* (to support a thing in an upward manner) is among the governing
principles taught toward nurturing hidden skills within Sun style taiji, bagua and xingyi.

Sun Lu-T'ang demonstrating Sun style taijiquan postures based upon creatures and Chinese deities.

太極拳

Sun Style Taiji Boxing 95-Posture Form

孫祿堂　原著　孫劍雲　整理

by Sun Jian-Yun, original material by Sun Lu-T'ang.

Published by 人民體育出版社 The People's Physical Education Press, September, 1957.

CONTENTS

Solo Form

Posture 37:　高探馬　High Explore [Test] Horse　(*Gau Tan Ma*)
Posture 38:　右起腳　Right Rising Foot　(*You Qi Jiao*)
Posture 39:　左起腳　Left Rising Foot　(*Zuo Qi Jiao*)
Posture 40:　轉身踢腳　Turn Body, Kick with Foot　(*Zhuan Shen Ti Jiao*)
Posture 41:　踐步打捶　Trampling Step, Hitting-Poundings　(*Jian Bu Da Ch'ui*)
Posture 42:　翻身二起　Overturn Body, Two Risings　(*Fan Shen Er Qi*)
Posture 43:　披身伏虎　Drape Body, Crouching Tiger　(*Pi Shen Fu Hu*)
Posture 44:　左踢腳　Left Kick with Foot　(*Zuo Ti Jiao*)
Posture 45:　右蹬腳　Right Pedaling Foot　(*You Deng Jiao*)
Posture 46:　上步搬攔捶　Step Up, Parry, Deflect, Pound [Beat]　(*Shang Bu Ban Lan Ch'ui*)
Posture 47:　如封似閉　Like Sealing, Appearing to Close　(*Ru Feng Si Bi*)
Posture 48:　抱虎推山　Embrace [Carry] Tiger, Push Mountain　(*Bao Hu Tui Shan*)
Posture 49:　開手　Open Hands　(*Kai Shou*)
Posture 50:　合手　Unite Hands　(*He'r Shou*)
Posture 51:　摟膝拗步　Brush Knee, Obstinate Step　(*Lo Xi Niu Bu*)
Posture 52:　懶扎衣　Lazily Tuck in Garment　(*Lan Zha Yi*)
Posture 53:　斜開手　Oblique [Diagonal] Open Hands　(*Xie Kai Shou*)
Posture 54:　斜合手　Oblique [Diagonal] Unite Hands　(*Xie He'r Shou*)
Posture 55:　斜單鞭　Oblique [Diagonal] Single Whip　(*Xie Dan Bien*)
Posture 56:　野馬分鬃　Wild Horse Separates Mane　(*Yeh Ma Fen Zong*)
Posture 57:　開手　Open Hands　(*Kai Shou*)
Posture 58:　合手　Unite Hands　(*He'r Shou*)
Posture 59:　單鞭　Single Whip　(*Dan Bien*)
Posture 60:　右通背掌　Right ~ Through Back Palm　(*You Tong Bei Zhang*)
Posture 61:　玉女穿梭　Jade Maiden Winds-Through Shuttle　(*Yu Nu Chuan Suo*)
Posture 62:　懶扎衣　Lazily Tuck in Garment　(*Lan Zha Yi*)
Posture 63:　開手　Open Hands　(*Kai Shou*)
Posture 64:　合手　Unite Hands　(*He'r Shou*)
Posture 65:　單鞭　Single Whip　(*Dan Bien*)
Posture 66:　雲手　Cloud Hands　(*Yun Shou*)
Posture 67:　雲手下勢　Cloud Hands Lower Posture　(*Yun Shou Xia Shi*)
Posture 68:　更雞獨立　Night-Watch Rooster Stands Alone　(*Ching [Geng] Chi Du Li*)
Posture 69:　倒攆猴　Collapse, Repulse Monkey　(*Dao Nian Hou*)
Posture 70:　手揮琵琶（右式）Hands Strum [Play] Lute ~ Right Style　(*Shou Wei Pipa ~ Zuo Shi*)
Posture 71:　白鶴亮翅　White Crane Displays [Shows] Wings　(*Bai He'r Liang Chr*)
Posture 72:　開手　Open Hands　(*Kai Shou*)
Posture 73:　合手　Unite Hands　(*He'r Shou*)
Posture 74:　摟膝拗步　Brush Knee, Obstinate Step　(*Lo Xi Niu Bu*)
Posture 75:　手揮琵琶　Hands Strum [Play] Lute　(*Shou Wei Pipa*)
Posture 76:　三通背　Three Through the Back　(*San Tong Bei*)
Posture 77:　開手　Open Hands　(*Kai Shou*)
Posture 78:　合手　Unite Hands　(*He'r Shou*)
Posture 79:　單鞭　Single Whip　(*Dan Bien*)
Posture 80:　雲手　Cloud Hands　(*Yun Shou*)
Posture 81:　高探馬　High Explore [Test] Horse　(*Gau Tan Ma*)
Posture 82:　十字擺蓮　Ten Character, Swing Lotus [Water Lily]　(*Shi Tze Bai Lien*)
Posture 83:　進步指襠捶　Advancing Step, Point [at] Crotch Pounding　(*Jin Bu Zhi Tang Ch'ui*)

太極拳

Sun Style Taiji Boxing 97-Posture Form

CONTENTS

Solo Form

Posture 26: 白鶴亮翅　White Crane Displays [Shows] Wings (*Bai He'r Liang Chr*)
Posture 27: 開手　Open Hands (*Kai Shou*)
Posture 28: 合手　Unite Hands (*He'r Shou*)
Posture 29: 摟膝拗步（左式）Brush Knee, Obstinate Step ~ Left Style (*Lo Xi Niu Bu ~ Zuo Shi*)
Posture 30: 手揮琵琶（左式）Hands Strum [Play] Lute ~ Left Style (*Shou Wei Pipa ~ Zuo Shi*)
Posture 31: 三通背　Three Through the Back (*San Tong Bei*)
Posture 32: 懶扎衣　Lazily Tuck in Garment (*Lan Zha Yi*)
Posture 33: 開手　Open Hands (*Kai Shou*)
Posture 34: 合手　Unite Hands (*He'r Shou*)
Posture 35: 單鞭　Single Whip (*Dan Bien*)
Posture 36: 雲手　Cloud Hands (*Yun Shou*)
Posture 37: 高探馬　High Explore [Test] Horse (*Gau Tan Ma*)
Posture 38: 右起腳　Right Rising Foot (*You Qi Jiao*)
Posture 39: 左起腳　Left Rising Foot (*Zuo Qi Jiao*)
Posture 40: 轉身踢腳　Turn Body, Kick with Foot (*Zhuan Shen Ti Jiao*)
Posture 41: 踐步打捶　Trampling Step, Hitting-Poundings (*Jian Bu Da Ch'ui*)
Posture 42: 翻身二起　Overturn Body, Two Risings (*Fan Shen Er Qi*)
Posture 43: 披身伏虎　Drape Body, Crouching Tiger (*Pi Shen Fu Hu*)
Posture 44: 左踢腳　Left Kick with Foot (*Zuo Ti Jiao*)
Posture 45: 右蹬腳　Right Pedaling Foot (*You Deng Jiao*)
Posture 46: 上步搬攔捶　Step Up, Parry, Deflect, Pound [Beat] (*Shang Bu Ban Lan Ch'ui*)
Posture 47: 如封似閉　Like Sealing, Appearing to Close (*Ru Feng Si Bi*)
Posture 48: 抱虎推山　Embrace [Carry] Tiger, Push Mountain (*Bao Hu Tui Shan*)
Posture 49: 開手　Open Hands (*Kai Shou*)
Posture 50: 合手　Unite Hands (*He'r Shou*)
Posture 51: 摟膝拗步　Brush Knee, Obstinate Step (*Lo Xi Niu Bu*)
Posture 52: 懶扎衣　Lazily Tuck in Garment (*Lan Zha Yi*)
Posture 53: 斜開手　Oblique [Diagonal] Open Hands (*Xie Kai Shou*)
Posture 54: 斜合手　Oblique [Diagonal] Unite Hands (*Xie He'r Shou*)
Posture 55: 斜單鞭　Oblique [Diagonal] Single Whip (*Xie Dan Bien*)
Posture 56: 野馬分鬃　Wild Horse Separates Mane (*Yeh Ma Fen Zong*)
Posture 57: 懶扎衣　Lazily Tuck in Garment (*Lan Zha Yi*)
Posture 58: 開手　Open Hands (*Kai Shou*)
Posture 59: 合手　Unite Hands (*He'r Shou*)
Posture 60: 單鞭　Single Whip (*Dan Bien*)
Posture 61: 右通背掌　Right ~ Through Back Palm (*You Tong Bei Zhang*)
Posture 62: 玉女穿梭　Jade Maiden Winds-Through Shuttle (*Yu Nu Chuan Suo*)
Posture 63: 懶扎衣　Lazily Tuck in Garment (*Lan Zha Yi*)
Posture 64: 開手　Open Hands (*Kai Shou*)
Posture 65: 合手　Unite Hands (*He'r Shou*)
Posture 66: 單鞭　Single Whip (*Dan Bien*)
Posture 67: 雲手　Cloud Hands (*Yun Shou*)
Posture 68: 雲手下勢　Cloud Hands Lower Posture (*Yun Shou Xia Shi*)
Posture 69: 更雞獨立　Night-Watch Rooster Stands Alone (*Ching* [*Geng*] *Chi Du Li*)
Posture 70: 倒攆猴　Collapse, Repulse Monkey (*Dao Nian Hou*)
Posture 71: 手揮琵琶（右式）Hands Strum [Play] Lute ~ Right Style (*Shou Wei Pipa ~ Zuo Shi*)
Posture 72: 白鶴亮翅　White Crane Displays [Shows] Wings (*Bai He'r Liang Chr*)
Posture 73: 開手　Open Hands (*Kai Shou*)

Posture 74: 合手 Unite Hands (*He'r Shou*)
Posture 75: 摟膝拗步 Brush Knee, Obstinate Step (*Lo Xi Niu Bu*)
Posture 76: 手揮琵琶 Hands Strum [Play] Lute (*Shou Wei Pipa*)
Posture 77: 三通背 Three Through the Back (*San Tong Bei*)
Posture 78: 懶扎衣 Lazily Tuck in Garment (*Lan Zha Yi*)
Posture 79: 開手 Open Hands (*Kai Shou*)
Posture 80: **合手** Unite Hands (*He'r Shou*)
Posture 81: 單鞭 Single Whip (*Dan Bien*)
Posture 82: 雲手 Cloud Hands (*Yun Shou*)
Posture 83: 高探馬 High Explore [Test] Horse (*Gau Tan Ma*)
Posture 84: 十字擺蓮 Ten Character, Swing Lotus [Water Lily] (*Shi Tze Bai Lien*)
Posture 85: 進步指襠捶 Advancing Step, Point [at] Crotch Pounding (*Jin Bu Zhi Tang Ch'ui*)
Posture 86: 退步懶扎衣 Withdrawing [Retreating] Step, Lazily Tuck in Garment (*Tui Bu Lan Zha Yi*)
Posture 87: **開手** Open Hands (*Kai Shou*)
Posture 88: 合手 Unite Hands (*He'r Shou*)
Posture 89: 單鞭 Single Whip (*Dan Bien*)
Posture 90: 單鞭下勢 Single Whip Lower Posture (*Dan Bien Xia Shi*)
Posture 91: 上步七星 Step Up [into the] Seven Stars (*Shang Bu Qi Xing*)
Posture 92: 退步跨虎 Withdrawing [Retreating] Step, Straddle Tiger (*Tui Bu Kua Hu*)
Posture 93: 轉角擺蓮 Turn to the Angle [Corner], Swing Lotus [Water Lily] (*Zhuan Jiao Bai Lien*)
Posture 94: 彎弓射虎 Bend Bow, Shoot Tiger (*Wan Gung She Hu*)
Posture 95: 雙撞捶 Double [Paired] Striking [Colliding] Poundings [Beatings] (*Shuang Zhuang Ch'ui*)
Posture 96: 陰陽混一 Yin-Yang Merge [Combine] into One [Oneness] (*Yin-Yang Hun Yi*)
Posture 97: 收式 Collecting [Receiving] Posture ~ Conclusion (*Shou Shi*)

太極拳
TAIJI BOXING

FORM
INSTRUCTION

起式 *Qi Shi*
Commencement [Beginning] Posture

Photo (1)   Photo (2)

Initial instructions that Madam Sun taught us in class concerning this section:

One's thoughts, emotions, and spirit draw inward to unite and harmonize. Sensing peacefulness and tranquility should be cultivated. These must be sought before proceeding, as they form the well-spring from which the correctness of movement finds its true root. Several minutes must be devoted to standing and entering into such harmony before movement is ensued. One's gaze is soft and receptive, peering levelly into *T'ai Kong* (the Great Void). Physically, an important aspect is now enacted, that is the crown point of the head must sense lifting upward while the jaw relaxes, the front teeth separate from the lower while the tip of the tongue rests upon the back of the upper front teeth. This now allows for the sensation of the area beneath the chin to sense heaviness. The head now mimics that of a mountain, drawing upward into a peak while spreading sinking-rootedness below. The head feels this manifestation first; this expression of *qi* spreads though one's trunk then, engulfs the entire body. Such manifestations are carried through the entirety of the *taiji* form from the commencement of the first posture.

Note: Quite often Madam Sun would repeat many important points when instructing us. My notes from those years reflect such redundancy, and because Madam Sun felt so strongly that such information be adhered to my writings, at times, will reflect such repetition of essential points.

Madam Sun told us that the very first posture in the *taiji* form 起式 *Qi Shi* (Commencement [Beginning] Posture) and the final posture 收式 *Shou Shi* (Collecting [Receiving] Posture) are the two most important postures as they establish the essence of *kai* and *he'r* carried throughout all successive movements. The first and final postures unite the 97 [95]-posture form into one continuously linked ring that has no beginning, no end, a reflection of the *Tai Kong* (the Great Void [the Cosmos]). However, the first posture is divided into two parts: Photo (1) and Photo (2), a reflection of *Yi* (Oneness) separating into *Liangyi* (Two Ones), this being the emergence of the *yin* and *yang*.

Photo (1):
One's thoughts, spirit and intent draw inward to unite and harmonize, merging with tranquility and the stirring of *qi*. These must be sought for some moments before proceeding, as these essentials form the well-spring from which the correctness of practice and movement find their true root. Devotion to such standing, entering into harmony before movement cannot be excluded should progress be sought. One's gaze is soft and receptive, peering levelly into *T'ai Kong* (the Great Void).

Important physical aspects that must be followed: the crown point of the head must sense drawing upward while the jaw relaxes downward; the front teeth separate from the lower while the tip of the tongue rests upon the back of the upper front teeth. These are to be conducted in unison. This now allows for the area beneath the chin to sense heaviness. Heaviness births lightness, this lightness being *yang qi* rising to the crown of the head, the area called *Niwan* (Mud Ball), where *yang* dictates the spreading of nimbleness and agility throughout the body. The head now mimics that of a mountain, drawing upward into a peak while spreading the sensation of *qi* sinking and rooting below. The head feels this manifestation first; this expression of *qi* spreads though one's trunk then, engulfing the entire body. As *yang qi* rises from one's back to *Niwan* (Mud Ball), it is vital that the tongue touches and lightly pushes upon the back of the upper front middle teeth [where teeth and gums meet] to enable *yang qi* to descend, and merge unfettered with *yin qi* in the front of one's body. In this manner, due to the tongue's great assistance, *qi* becomes unified, vibrant and enhanced within. Simultaneously, as the tongue touches behind the upper front teeth, one's perineum softly draws inward, assisting yin qi to stream upward where it conjoins with yang qi. These two corporeal actions, the touching of the tongue and the drawing in of the perineum, assist and bolster the *yin* and *yang* in the process of *hua* (transforming) into a unified force.

The middle fingers touch upon the center line of the lower legs. This establishes unity between upper [the arms] and lower [the legs]; the inside [of the arms] with the outside [of the legs]], bringing these four together to create the 四合, 合一氣 *si he'r, he'r yi qi* (four unifications, unify into one *qi*).

The inner regions of the heels of both feet touch to establish connective *qi* with the *Yongquan* (Gushing Spring) points at the bottoms of the feet; from there *qi* rises through the body's core to the crown of one's head. This posture is the means by which *yin* below conjoins with *yang* above, transforming into that which embraces all parts of one's body, a connective web of *qi* .

Below is a related question that we asked Madam Sun that specifically addresses the acu-points: *Yongquan* (Gushing Spring) and *Niwan* (Mud Ball), also known as *Baihui* (Hundred Meetings).

Q: Students have commented that sometimes they feel heavy and clumsy, and other times light and without balance. Would you explain these phenomena, and what should be done to overcome such extremes?

A: When one senses the body becoming light, this can indicate advancement. Lightness of one's *qi* means that it is purified and in harmony with the *qi* of nature. However, should you sense that your body is light and without *zhongdin* (central equilibrium) this is an indication that one's interior *qi* is moving like a gusting wind that has no root, this being ill in nature. Floating imbalance can be remedied through placing one's intent at *Yongquan* (Gushing Spring), at the bottom of both feet. Each point unites with the heavy, rooted *qi* of the Earth. Should a person feel overly heavy and sluggish in movement, then one should concentrate upon *Baihui* (Hundred Meetings), where *yang qi* converges, rises and unites with Heaven.

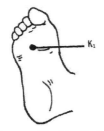
Yongquan (Gushing Spring)

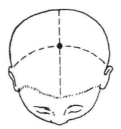
Baihui (Hundred Meetings)

四象 *Si Xiang* ~ The Four Resemblances:

When standing, as in Posture 1, or moving throughout the 97-posture form, the 四象 *Si Xiang* (Four Resemblances) are constantly adhered to and simultaneously performed:

1. 象鷄腿 *Xiang Ji Tui* (Resembling a Rooster's Leg) ~ this is the shape that one's body assumes when standing upon a single leg. Such a posture mimics the standing of a rooster that has raised a single leg with the purpose of 'about to move.' Raising a single leg must have intent beyond merely raising. Raising one leg requires the supporting leg to sink, establishing the foundation and stability from which to 'rise.' This is the dualism of movement among the *yin* and *yang*, upper and lower giving birth to and support to the other. 象鷄腿 *Xiang Ji Tui* (Resembling a Rooster's Leg), therefore, is not merely the standing upon

a single leg; it is the overall concept of simultaneously rising and sinking in a unified manner while maintaining one's central equilibrium. Whether the leg rises into a kick, rises to assume a standing posture or rises very slightly with the toes touching lightly upon the ground, all are postures conforming to principles contained within Rooster Leg training. Furthermore, 鷄 *ji* (rooster) signifies the heralding of *yang* essence and hence the inception of movement. Movement of one's body stems from the wellspring of the feet [referring to the *Yongquan* (Gushing Spring) point] and legs, one side sensing rootedness and contraction, the other sensing lightness and extension. The earth's *qi* enters through both feet and rises to the crown of one's head [referring to *Baihui* (Hundred Meetings) point], along this journey the primordial essence is dispersed through the limbs and organs. To raise one leg like a rooster heralding the dawn enhances *qi* to surge to the crown-point from where it unifies the all things within one's interior. This is the meaning of 象鷄腿 *Xiang Ji Tui* (Resembling a Rooster's Leg) as taught by Master Sun Lu-T'ang.

2. 象龍身 *Xiang Lung Shen* (Resembling a Dragon's Body) ~ a dragon's limbs embrace strength from the innate skill of using the 三折 *San Zhe* (Three Bends [Breaks]): the bending found in the inner hip region [outer pelvic area], the bending of the knees and the bending of the ankles. These three bends act as bows about to release an arrow of force. Each bow is likened to a storehouse of strength, accumulating, enhancing, and sustaining itself.

3. 象熊膀 *Xiang Xiong Bang* (Resembling a Bear's Shoulders) ~ the neck maintains an upright position enabling *qi* to follow a vertical pathway to the crown of one's head. Further, one's shoulders sense roundness and fullness, enabling the shoulders to roll like a great bear's girth in movement. *Xiong Bang* (Bear Shoulders) unifies both the shoulders and neck, hence are considered as one. The shoulders are mirrors of below, that being one's hips.

4. 象虎抱頭 *Xiang Hu Bao Tou* (Resembling a Tiger Embracing [Its] Head) ~one's body crouches like a tiger preparing to leap from its lair, while the arms and paws of a tiger extend as if to embrace and cover its head in a protective manner. The tips of the fingers, which resemble the outstretched claws of a tiger, lead and merge with one's 心 *xin* (heart [the mind]) and 意 *yi* (intent) to produce 力 *li* (force). This is one meaning of 象虎抱頭 *Xiang Hu Bao Tou* (Resembling a Tiger Embracing [Its] Head).

懶扎衣 *Lan Zha Yi*
Lazily Tuck in Garment

Photo (3)

Photo (4)

Photo (5)

Photo (6)

Photo (7)

Photo (8)

Photo (9)

Photo (10)

Below is a question that we asked Madam Sun, as it is directly related to the importance of fingertips in each posture, specifically, in this case, concerning the set of movements within 懶扎衣 *Lan Zha Yi* (Lazily Tuck in Garment). She quickly commented that Lazily Tuck in Garment follows the principles dictated within 象虎抱頭 *Xiang Hu Bao Tou* (Resembling a Tiger Embracing [Its] Head).

Q: What is the importance of keeping the finger tips pointing upwards or forwards during certain postures?

A: Upon the tip of each of the ten fingers lies a point where *qi* pools and achieves wondrous acts. These ten points are known as the *Shi Xuan* (Ten Proclamations). Master Sun highly emphasized them during practice. When the Ten Proclamations face upward, as in: Single Whip, *Kai-Shou, He'r-Shou*, turbid *qi* is expelled [proclaimed outwardly, as if announcing), bringing the interior back into harmony. As the Ten face any direction, *qi* extends, then reverts back within the body.

Note: In practicing many postures the fingers point one direction while the thumbs spread open to establish the formation of a 'Tiger's Mouth.' Though the *Shi Xuan* do not all physically point the same direction, it is eight fingers that shall, with the thumbs being the exception. It is one's *yi* (mind-intent) that unifies the purpose of the *Shi Xuan*.

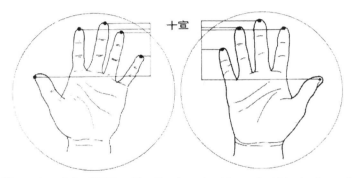

Illustration of the *Shi Xuan* (Ten Proclamations) located within the finger tips.

The *Shi Xuan* (Ten Proclamations) are like ten stars moving among 天漢 *Tian Han* (Heaven's Moving Sand [known in the West as the Milky Way]. In *neijiaquan*, postures endlessly move together as one, there is no separation from beginning to end. It is as if gazing upon stars that harmoniously move within the 天漢 *Tian Han*.

Note: The character 漢 *Han* comes from the radicals '*water*' and '*do not*.' The meaning of 漢, in the context above, is: moving sands; a sandy plain. Therefore, 天漢 *Tian Han* refers to 'sand moving [like tiny stars] among Heaven.'

As the *Shi Xuan* move their purpose is enhanced by four principles [actions] that are carried throughout all practices of sitting, standing, individual postures, solo forms, partner forms, weaponry and *qigong*. These four are: *t'i* (rise), *luo* (fall/drop), *kai* (open) and *he'r* (unite [close]). Movement and *yi* (mind-intent) that 'rise' empower one's *qi* and *shen* (will) to ascend and thereby flourish throughout the four limbs and body's surface. That which 'falls' descends into cultivating rootedness, thereby drawing turbid *qi* downward, leaving behind purified *qi* within the organs. To 'open' expands and spreads *qi* and spirit throughout, thereby banishing impure *qi* [illness]. To 'unite [close]' inwardly draws the 五行 *wuxing* (five elements) into a state of *hua* (transformation), from which the four principles [actions] stem.

Examples of some postures in which the *Shi Xuan* (Ten Proclamations) are especially emphasized.

Sun Lu-T'ang demonstrating the *Si Xuan* (Ten Proclamations) principle of practice.

開手 *Kai Shou*
Open Hands

Photo (11)

合手 *He'r Shou*
Unite Hands

Photo (12)

單鞭 *Dan Bien*
Single Whip

Photo (13)

It was a very brisk morning in Beijing in 1985, Madam Sun had just arrived at class and said that she wanted to explain the meaning of 單鞭 *Dan Bien* (Single Whip). I had already learned the fundamentals of this posture from her the previous year, but she felt that it was time for many of us to learn the original meaning. One of my classmates translated much of the lecture for me because Madam Sun had used words colloquial to the Beijing dialect and old terminology from her father's generation. As if this was not difficult enough to tackle Madam Sun requested that I refer to several of the old dictionaries on Chinese written characters to gain further insights into the separate characters of 單 *Dan* (Single) and 鞭 *Bien* (Whip). She asked that I take detailed notes in my class notebook so that she could see this later. Though I wrote nearly all of my notes in English at that time she still wanted to see how thoroughly I researched these two simple characters. This was not a test on her part, but rather observing my motivation to learn, and to what depth. Over the years Madam Sun taught profound aspects of Single Whip which clarified its great importance in the practice of *taijiquan*. These aspects will be covered in another of our books. However, among the most important facets that she taught was that Single Whip teaches the application of the principles: *四平式 *Si P'ing Shi* (Four Equals Posture), 太開手 *T'ai Kai Shou* (Great Open Hands), and 雙劈掌 *Shuang P'i Zhang* (Double [Paired] Splitting Palm). Together these principles, of which 四平式 *Si P'ing Shi* (Four Equals Posture) is emphasized, culminate in stretching open, in a very soft manner, all expanses of the body into which *qi* shall permeate.

*Note: 四平式 *Si P'ing Shi* (Four Equals Posture) refers to both arms and both legs being used equally according to strength in movement. The character 平 *p'ing* is composed of the radicals *in* and *eight*. Together these radicals express the meaning: even, level, equal, uniform, peaceful, tranquil, quiet, to restore quiet. In Chinese boxing, particularly regarding *taijiquan*, *baguazhang*, and *xingyiquan*, the term 四平 *si p'ing* refers to 'four things that remain equal [level, even] in their use of intent, strength and spirit. The fingers and toes all express outward as a collective whole in accord with the principle of *kai* (to open); likewise they collectively draw inward, as if slightly clutching in accord with the principle of *he'r* (to unite, close). Such principles involve the entirety of one's body. Master Sun Lu-T'ang taught that it is best to initially confine such practice to both hands and both feet, placing great emphasis upon the fingers and toes. In time, the four limbs, as well as all regions of the body, become immersed within these principles. It is at that point that the 四平 *si p'ing* (four equals), in all standing, lying, and sitting movement, will begin to be understood in part.

Regarding 鞭 *bien* (whip), the original root character (*ko* [*koh*]) represents the look of a raw skin, either animal or human, as it is stretched out with the hair scraped off to change its appearance. With horns or ears on top, the body's trunk flayed open and the legs stretched aside while the tail is drawn out, the skin is taut in all directions. It therefore expresses stretching outwardly; the idea that change takes place, and that of renewal. The skin is not of the type that is cured or dressed, which indicates an immediate action has taken place. This root character further means: to put off; reject; to change; an ancient defensive armor; and the head of a bridle.

Madam Sun taught that this root character further denotes the meaning that the four limbs must equally stretch, not one must lack in essence. To stretch does not merely mean to physically feel tautness, but the spirit of stretching outwardly must be sensed within the four limbs. Upper and lower mirror one another and simultaneously conjoin in motion and stillness. These concepts are commonly expressed within the term *四平式 *Si P'ing Shi* (Four Equals Posture) which is to be followed within every posture. *Si P'ing Tui Shou* (Four Equals Push Hands) is an applied practice taught within each branch of traditional *taijiquan*.

The complete character directly above is *bien* (a whip or whipping action; a lash or lashing action). However, to translate *bien* as merely a whip, or to whip does not show the depth of its true meaning. The right half of the character 鞭 is composed of the root radicals of *man* and *to change*. Together these two radicals mean to alter one's inconvenient position, and assume one that is most advantageous. In performing the movement *Dan Bien* (Single Whip) you must seek a position in which one's *zhong din* (central equilibrium) is uncompromised through attaining an advantageous position. Advantageous refers to moving and stretching into a defensive posture and position in which I am able to control an adversary and his intent. Stretching outwardly is the mutual blending of *kai* (to open) and *jin* (expressed force) in all striking and defensive arm methods, and within all stepping and kicking methods, no matter having emerged from an offensive or defensive nature.

Bien (to whip; a lash: to flog; to whip a lash; a cut or stroke of a whip; to flog) also had a somewhat different meaning through the centuries. This character referred to an iron bludgeon, a rod of wood or iron, and flogging as a punishment inflicted upon government officers. However, Madam Sun said that during her father's generation many of the elder boxing masters taught that the older form of 鞭 came from the meanings *to enter* and *to stroke*. The encompassing meaning was, therefore, to enter into an advantageous position through using a stroking action as if to use a whip or rod of wood or iron.

Regarding 劈掌 *P'i Zhang* (Splitting Palm):

It is important to understand the meaning of the character 劈 (*p'i*). The character 劈 comes from the radicals: *knife* and *a sovereign or prince*. Together these radicals [root parts of each written character] express the meanings: to rend or split open, to cut open, to divide, to tear asunder, to wedge, wedge-shaped. *Sovereign* comes from a heavenly source, and being the offspring of the Son of Heaven [the Emperor] denotes that all things associated with 劈 shall invoke the 五行者金木水火土 *wuxing: jin, mu, shui, huo, tu* (five elements: gold [metal], wood, water, fire, and earth) which stir and transform within one's movements toward attaining 合一氣 *he'r yi qi* (unification into one *qi*).

Madam Sun said 'My father's *xingyiquan* teacher, Master Guo Yun-Shen, taught that 劈 *p'i* (splitting) must be learned and practiced before all other sets, as it is the root from which the *xingyi* cycle begins. 'Root' refers to the source from which all organs receive their perpetual well-spring of *qi* and movement. 'Cycle' refers to the five fists and twelve animal sets harmonizing and acting as a waterwheel that churns one's *qi* and spirit within one's being. Each fistic set, each animal when practiced, is like a paddle upon the waterwheel, moving and strengthening the wheel's influence. 劈掌 *P'i Zhang* (Splitting Palm) is paired with the element *jin* (gold [generally referred to as metal]. Its *qi* is rooted and expressed through and from the lungs into the body's Great Cycle [the wheel of *qi* that perpetually revolves]. This is attained through the precise movement of this hand method, likened to that of a heavy sharp blade; suddenly dropping as if an axe from Heaven that 劈 *p'i* (splits, renders) through all that it touches. As one's hand rises from below, reaching upward toward Heaven to unite with *yang qi*, the *nei shen qi* (the body's internal energy) rises upward to the top of one's head. As one's hand drops like an axe it 劈 *p'i* (splits, renders) directly downward without the slightest deviation, as does one's *qi*. This is one of several methods to be practiced.'

提手上式 *T'i Shou Shang Shi*
Lift Hands Upward Posture

Photo (14)

白鶴亮翅 *Bai He'r Liang Chr*
White Crane Displays [Shows] Wings

Photo (15)   Photo (16)   Photo (17)

開手 *Kai Shou*
Open Hands

Photo (18)

Posture 9

合手 *He'r Shou*
Unite Hands

Photo (19)

摟膝拗步（左式）*Lo Xi Niu Bu ~ Zuo Shi*
Brush Knee, Obstinate Step ~ Left Style

Photo (20)   Photo (21)

Posture 11

手揮琵琶（左式）*Shou Wei Pipa ~ Zuo Shi*
Hands Strum [Play] Lute ~ Left Style

Photo (22)

進步搬攔捶 *Jin Bu Ban Lan Ch'ui*
Advancing Step, Parry, Deflect, Pound [Beat]

Photo (23)

Photo (24)

Photo (25)

Photo (26)

如封似閉 *Ru Feng Si Bi*
Like Sealing, Appearing to Close

Photo (27)

抱虎推山 *Bao Hu Tui Shan*
Carry [Embrace] Tiger, Push Mountain

Photo (28)

開手 *Kai Shou*
Open Hands

Photo (29)

合手 *He'r Shou*
Unite Hands

Photo (30)

摟膝拗步（右式）*Lo Xi Niu Bu ~ You Shi*

Brush Knee, Obstinate Step Posture ~ Right Style

Photo (31) Photo (32)

懶扎衣 *Lan Zha Yi*
Lazily Tuck Garment

Photo (33) Photo (34) Photo (35)

Photo (36) Photo (37) Photo (38)

開手 *Kai Shou*
Open Hands

Photo (39)

合手 *He'r Shou*
Unite Hands

Photo (40)

Posture 21

單鞭 *Dan Bien*
Single Whip

Photo (41)

Posture 22

肘下看捶 *Zhou Xia Kan Ch'ui*
Beneath the Elbow Guarding [Watching] Strike [Beat]

Photo (42)

倒攆猴（左式）*Dao Nian Hou ~ Zuo Shi*
Collapse [Step Back], Repulse Monkey ~ Left Style

[Sitting-Back Step (Collapse), Repulse Monkey]

Photo (43)   Photo (44)

Posture 24

倒攆猴（右式）*Dao Nian Hou ~ You Shi*
Collapse [Step Back], Repulse Monkey ~ Right Style

[Sitting-Back Step (Collapse), Repulse Monkey]

Photo (45)   Photo (46)

手揮琵琶（右式）*Shou Wei Pipa ~ Zuo Shi*
Hands Strum [Play] Lute ~ Right Style

Photo (47)

白鶴亮翅 *Bai He'r Liang Chr*
White Crane Displays [Shows] Wings

Photo (48)   Photo (49)   Photo (50)

開手 *Kai Shou*
Open Hands

Photo (51)

合手 *He'r Shou*
Unite Hands

Photo (52)

摟膝拗步（左式）*Lo Xi Niu Bu ~ Zuo Shi*
Brush Knee, Obstinate Step ~ Left Style

Photo (53)   Photo (54)

Posture 30

手揮琵琶（左式）*Shou Wei Pipa ~ Zuo Shi*
Hands Strum [Play] Lute ~ Left Style

Photo (55)

三通背 *San T'ong Bei*
Three Through the Back

Photos (56-63)

懒扎衣 *Lan Zha Yi*
Lazily Tuck Garment

Photo (64)

Photo (65)

Photo (66)

Photo (67)

開手 *Kai Shou*
Open Hands

Photo (68)

合手 *He'r Shou*
Unite Hands

Photo (69)

單鞭 *Dan Bien*
Single Whip

Photo (70)

雲手 *Yun Shou*
Cloud Hands

Photo (71)   Photo (72)

高探馬 *Gau Tan Ma*
High Explore [Test] Horse

Photo (73)   Photo (74)   Photo (75)

Posture 38

右起腳 *You Qi Jiao*
Right Rising Foot

Photo (76)

Posture 39

左起腳 *Zuo Qi Jiao*

Left Rising Foot

Photo (77)

Posture 40

轉身踢腳 *Zhuan Shen Ti Jiao*

Turn Body, Kick with Foot

NO PHOTO

Note: In 1956, Madam Sun was photograph performing each of the postures for this book. She edited through the photos and selected only those which passed her critique. When the book was printed one photo was extremely blurred in many of the printed copies. The print shop, with her permission, decided that removing that photo would be best in quickly completing the printing of the remaining books. Retaking the photo and inserting it would take additional time that Madam Sun felt was unnecessary and would cause the printer trouble. She had decided that the explanation of how to perform the posture was sufficient for general practice. Specifically, Madam Sun had told us to refer to Xu Yu-

Sheng's 1927 book *Taijiquan Shi* (Tai-Chi Boxing Power Enhancement) concerning this posture. Master Xu, detailed in my translation of his book, had hired Sun Lu-T'ang at several of his large teaching institutions in Beijing. Their many years of cooperative teaching programs to bring traditional martial and health practices to the public brought both of them popular acclaim. Below is an abstract from Xu's 1927 book concerning the same method taught by Master Sun and Madam Sun Jian-Yun under the posture name 轉身踢腳 *Zhuan Shen Ti Jiao* (Turn Body, Kick with Foot).

轉身蹬腳式

Turn Body, Stepping Upon with Foot Posture
[Turn Body and Pedal-Kick with Heel]
Zhuan Shen Deng Jiao Shr

Explanation of the Posture's Name:
轉身蹬腳 *Zhuan Shen Deng* Jiao* refers to the body turning to face rearward, then kicking with the heel, followed by stepping forward upon the ground with one's heel. The movement is likened to the swirling of a dragon that rises and lashes outward with a whipping action.

The Two Actions Contained Within:
1. *Zhuan Shen* (Turn Body).
2. *Deng* Jiao* (Stepping Upon with Foot [Pedaling Foot]).

*蹬 *Deng* means to 'step upon' or 'to pedal' according to classical old Chinese characters. Master Chen Wei-Ming taught that in *taijiquan* its action is like that of climbing a hill in which you must raise the leg, extend it forth, and step down with the heel leading the planting action of the *jiao* (foot). Therefore, *deng* has come to mean using one's heel in an extending fashion, as if to kick or to pounce down upon using the foot, emphasizing use of the heel.

圖式腳蹬身轉

Turn Body, Stepping Upon with Foot Posture.

Explanation of the Illustration:
1. *Shou zuo zu* (The left foot receives [weight is unloaded into the left foot as it withdraws]). The toes touch the ground, and as the body turns leftward the right foot supports one's body to maintain a standing upright position. Concurrently, both arms move from an outward position to slightly lowering into an inward facing embrace [both palms face one's body as if embracing]. Both wrists touch to create *Shi Tze Shou Shi* (Ten Character Hands Posture). One's entire right side: neck, back, arm, leg, and foot are slightly curved [rounded] as the whole body slightly lowers into a sitting [squatting] position. As the left foot's toes touch the ground, one's eyes look [gaze] leftward.
2. As one's body rises, *shuang shou zuo you fen kai* (both hands, the left and right, separate open). Concurrently, the left foot raises, prepares, and faces leftward, executing a direct *deng* (stepping upon) action. It is the *zu zhong* (foot's heel) that issues [expresses] power in making contact with the adversary.

Points of Special Attention *&* Annotations:
As you turn the body you must stand upright [straight] and not lean or fall forward. One's ankles, knees and hips move as a dragon stretching and twisting its legs. The hands and arms must not be aimlessly flailed as they contract and expand with explosive force. The fingers, nose and toes must align without hindrance. Rolling inward and rolling outward is the secret to follow. The waist is the wheel's pivot from which roundness, body unity, and effortless motion are born. *Qi* that is drawn inward and held below shall find its mirrored action in expanding and exploding upward. Stillness within shall manifest the attainment of spontaneous outward movement. A single unified action is the harmony of movement within. Gather into a single force all the actions contained within this posture and the five directions and eight winds are at your command. Its secret of power is not within the kick, but hides within the methods of attainment.

Application:
Should an adversary, who is behind my body, suddenly strike at me, I should turn my body to apply the skill *bi guo** (evade-passing by). This presents the opportunity for me to kick, using *deng jiao* (stepping upon with the foot). Simultaneously with the kick, both hands spread facing to the left and right using the skill *fen-kai* (separate-open). This action thwarts the adversary from brushing my leg away [pitching my leg to the side].

**Bi* here means to 'avoid or evade' danger by turning the body away from a strike. Guo, in this context, means to 'pass by' an incoming strike, thereby avoiding the hit. Therefore, *bi guo* refers to the ability of maneuvering one's body [turning, dodging, shifting, and so forth] to evade and pass by [to clear away from] an attack.

踐步打捶 *Jian Bu Da Ch'ui*
Trampling Step, Hitting-Strikes

Photo (78)   Photo (79)

Photo (80)   Photo (81)

翻身二起 *Fan Shen Er Qi*
Overturn Body, Two Risings

Photo (82)

Photo (83)

Photo (84)

Photo (85)

Photo (86)

披身伏虎 *Pi Shen Fu Hu*
Drape Body, Crouching Tiger

Photo (87)   Photo (88)   Photo (89)

Posture 44

左踢腳 *Zuo Ti Jiao*
Left Kick with Foot

Photo (90)

右蹬腳 *You Deng Jiao*
Right Pedaling Foot

Photo (91)   Photo (92)

Photo (93)

上步搬攔捶 *Shang Bu Ban Lan Ch'ui*
Step Up [Advance], Parry, Deflect, Pound [Beat]

Photo (94)   Photo (95)   Photo (96)

如封似閉 *Ru Feng Si Bi*
Like Sealing, Appearing to Close

Photo (97)

抱虎推山 *Bao Hu Tui Shan*
Carry [Embrace] Tiger, Push Mountain

Photo (98)

開手 *Kai Shou*
Open Hands

Photo (99)

合手 *He'r Shou*
Unite Hands

Photo (100)

摟膝拗步 *Lo Xi Niu Bu*
Brush Knee, Obstinate Step

Photo (101)   Photo (102)

懒扎衣 *Lan Zha Yi*
Lazily Tuck Garment

Photos (103-108)

斜開手 *Xie Kai Shou*
Oblique [Diagonal] Open Hands

Photo (109)

斜合手 *Xie He'r Shou*
Oblique [Diagonal] Unite Hands

Photo (110)

斜單鞭 *Xie Dan Bien*
Oblique [Diagonal] Single Whip

Photo (111)

野馬分鬃 *Yeh Ma Fen Zong*
Wild Horse Separates [Parts] Mane

Photos (112-121)

開手 *Kai Shou*
Open Hands

Photo (122)

合手 *He'r Shou*
Unite Hands

Photo (123)

Posture 59

單鞭 *Dan Bien*
Single Whip

Photo (124)

Posture 60

右通背掌 *You Tong Bei Zhang*
Right ~ Through the Back Palm

Photo (125)

玉女穿梭 *Yu Nu Chuan Suo*
Jade Maiden Winds-Through Shuttle

Photos (126-132)

懒扎衣 *Lan Zha Yi*
Lazily Tuck in Garment

Photos (133-138)

開手 *Kai Shou*
Open Hands

Photo (139)

合手 *He'r Shou*
Unite Hands

Photo (140)

單鞭 *Dan Bien*
Single Whip

Photo (141)

雲手 *Yun Shou*
Cloud Hands

Photo (142)   Photo (143)

雲手下勢 *Yun Shou Xia Shi*
Cloud Hands Lower Posture

Photo (144)

Photo (145)

Photo (146)

更雞獨立 *Ching [Geng] Chi Du Li Zhang*
Night-Watch Rooster Stands Alone

Photo (147)   Photo (148)

倒攆猴 *Dao Nian Hou*
Collapse [Step Back], Repulse Monkey

[Sitting-Back Step (Collapse), Repulse Monkey]

Photos (149-!52)

手揮琵琶（右式）*Shou Wei Pipa ~ Zuo Shi*
Hands Strum [Play] Lute ~ Right Style

Photo (153)

白鶴亮翅 *Bai He'r Liang Chr*
White Crane Displays [Shows] Wings

Photo (154)   Photo (155)   Photo (156)

開手 *Kai Shou*
Open Hands

Photo (157)

合手 *He'r Shou*
Unite Hands

Photo (158)

摟膝拗步 *Lo Xi Niu Bu*
Brush Knee, Obstinate Step

Photo (159)   Photo (160)

Posture 75

手揮琵琶 *Shou Wei Pipa*
Hands Strum [Play] Lute

Photo (161)

三通背 *San Tong Bei*
Three Through the Back

Photos (162-173)

開手 *Kai Shou*
Open Hands

Photo (174)

Posture 78

合手 *He'r Shou*
Unite Hands

Photo (175)

單鞭 *Dan Bien*
Single Whip

Photo (176)

雲手 *Yun Shou*
Cloud Hands

Photo (177)　　　　　　　　　Photo (178)

高探馬 *Gau Tan Ma*
High Explore [Test] Horse

Photo (179-182)

十字擺蓮 *Shi Tze Bai Lien*
Ten Character, Swing Lotus [Water Lily]

Photo (183)

進步指襠捶 *Jin Bu Zhi Tang Ch'ui*
Advancing Step, Point [at] Crotch Pounding

Photo (184)

退步懶扎衣 *Tui Bu Lan Zha Yi*
Withdrawing Step, Lazily Tuck Garment

Photo (185)　　　　　　　Photo (186)　　　　　　　Photo (186)

Posture 85

開手 *Kai Shou*

Open Hands

Photo (187)

Posture 86

合手 *He'r Shou*

Unite Hands

Photo (188)

單鞭 *Dan Bien*
Single Whip

Photo (189)

單鞭下勢 *Dan Bien Xia Shi*
Single Whip Lower Posture

Photo (190)

上步七星 *Shang Bu Qi Xing*
Step Up [into the] Seven Stars

Photo (191)

退步跨虎 *Tui Bu Kua Hu*
Withdrawing [Retreating] Step, Straddle Tiger

Photo (192)   Photo (193)

Posture 91

轉角擺蓮 *Zhuan Jian Bai Lien*

Turn to the Angle [Corner], Swing Lotus [Water Lily]

Photo (195)   Photo (196)

Posture 92

彎弓射虎 *Wan Gung She Hu*

Bend Bow, Shoot Tiger

Photo (197)

雙撞捶 *Shuang Zhuang Ch'ui*
Double Striking [Colliding] Poundings [Beatings]

Photo (198)   Photo (199)

陰陽混一 *Yin-Yang Hun Yi*
Yin~Yang Merge [Combine] into Oneness

Photo (200)   Photo (201)

收式 *Shou Shi*
Collecting [Receiving] Posture
Conclusion

Photo (202)

Taoist Song [Poem]

by

Chi K'ang (A.D. 223-262)

*I will cast out Wisdom and reject learning.
My thoughts shall wander in the Great Void.
Always repenting of wrongs done
Will never, bring my heart to rest.
I cast my hook in a single stream;
But my joy is as though I possess a Kingdom.
I loose my hair and go singing;
To the four frontiers men join in my refrain.
This is the purport of my song:
"My thoughts shall wander in the Great Void."

*Source: *A Hundred & Seventy Chinese Poems.*
Published: May, 1919. Translator: Arthur Waley

www.neijiabooks.com

45237597R00053

Made in the USA
Middletown, DE
28 June 2017